Linux:

2019 NEW Easy User Manual to Learn the Linux Operating System and Linux Command Line

ISBN: 9781072003144

CONTENTS

Thank you for purchasing this book!

We always try to give more value then you expect. That's why we've updated the content and you can get it for FREE. You can get the digital version for free because you bought the print version.

The book is under the match program from Amazon. You can find how to do this using next URL: https://www.amazon.com/gp/digital/ep-landing-page

I hope it will be useful for you.

Introduction

Linux is the operating system, which today is actually the only alternative replacement for Windows from Microsoft.

Linux originates from 1991 when a young programmer from Finland Linus Torvalds took up work on the very first version of the system, which was named after him. The dawn of Linux's popularity began with its inception. This is due, primarily, to the fact that the core of this OS, like most programs written for it, has very important qualities.

There are many versions of Linux, for example, Linux - Unix, Debian, Mint, Ubuntu, OpenSUSE, and Gentoo.

Linux is a Unix-like operating system created and distributed in accordance with the free and open source software development model. Linux systems are widely used in the market of smartphones and server hardware. However, a considerable number of ordinary home users prefer the Linux family of MS Windows operating systems.

A feature of the Linux system is the lack of a single distribution. Multiple versions of Linux, such as Debian, Mint, Ubuntu, OpenSUSE, Gentoo, etc., are being developed in parallel by various development commands.

The client terminal can be installed and used on computers running the Ubuntu operating system using Wine. Wine is free software that allows users of Unix-like systems to run applications developed for Microsoft Windows systems. Among others, there is also a version of Wine for Ubuntu.

Chapter 1 - What is Linux and Why Use It?

Let's see, and why, in fact, Linux is needed for an ordinary person, not a computer fan and not a hacker. Let's start with the advantages of Linux:

1. Free. The Linux distribution can be downloaded from the

Internet, burned to DVD or CD and, after booting from this disc, can be installed.

2. Any Linux distribution already contains all the programs imaginable for the average user: text editors, word processors, programs for working with images of any complexity, several browsers, the whole range of Internet applications such as Skype, Messengers and other installation tools and removal programs, splitting hard drives into sections, dictionaries, simple games like solitaire and Tetris, and so much more. All this is not necessary to purchase and install, it is installed automatically with the operating system. And it takes along with the system no more than 10 GB of disk space.

3. Linux is designed for local area networks and for the Internet. It works faster, is more reliable and has one giant advantage – invulnerability to viruses. More precisely, a little more than a hundred viruses are known for Linux, and greedy collectors exchange them like rare butterflies. Accordingly, you do not have to install and update the antivirus on a weekly basis, reinstall Windows, when it simply stops working under the onslaught of viruses, overpay for Internet traffic, when viruses start sending spam from all over the world.

For the sake of objectivity, let us talk about the main disadvantages of Linux:

1. Extreme diversity and a rich selection of obscure for neophyte options: many distributions, many programs, many file systems, and lots of unsystematized and often outdated information.

2. The difficulty of exchanging programs between different distributions. A newbie is forced to use those programs that are offered by the program repository of this distribution.

3. Unfortunately, Linux does not work or works very poorly, with complex modern games. Not long ago, the main difficulty was installing Linux on your computer; Now with many distributions,

this procedure is simpler than installing Windows. Extremely common is the so-called LiveCD, which allows you to run the Linux distribution directly from a CD or from a DVD and try it out. The hard disk of your computer does not participate in this. And if you need to save something, then save it to a USB flash drive. But enough pros and cons, it's time to answer the main question: "Why?" Before answering it, you should understand that Linux is a very friendly system in relation to Windows. To install Linux, you do not need a separate computer, or even a separate hard drive (hard disk), you need only a bit of free space on a computer with a Windows operating system. This requires 10-15 gigabytes of free disk space. With modern disk sizes, this is quite a bit. When working together, Linux and Windows do not have any problems. Windows simply does not see the partition occupied by Linux. And Linux knows perfectly well where Windows is lying, allows you to read and modify Windows files and folders, copy them and share data with Windows. So, in case of problems with Windows, Linux will save valuable files from the Windows partition. Moreover, it installs its boot loader and will load Windows first if you want. When the time comes to reinstall Windows, the new version will overwrite the Linux boot loader and install Windows. But this is not a problem, Linux can be run from a flash drive, from a CD. After running Linux, you can easily restore its boot loader, allowing you to load any number of operating systems. So, we got close to the answer. There is no need to decide whether to switch to Linux or stay in Windows. You can simply have a second Linux operating system on the same hard disk. If you're using Linux, it is convenient to access the Internet, receive and send mail, upload and send programs and other files, use Skype; use the communication capabilities available on your computer. everything connected with the risk of infecting a computer with a virus should be done with the Linux operating system. Linux is very well written: its text editors are rich in useful tools, and they are fast and easy. But if you need Word, then copy the text file to the "territory" of Windows and enjoy your favorite processor. Even under Windows, it is better to work in programs like Photoshop,

Macromedia Flash, Corel Draw and the like – under Linux, they do not work. If you use Microsoft Office, then do it in your native environment. The same applies to games. Thus, you will protect yourself from viruses and gradually master another operating system, a skill that is reasonably useful. And for a snack, I would venture to advise the distribution, which is ideal for the scheme I described. This is the most popular Linux distribution around the world – Ubuntu. I just download the latest version, today it is Ubuntu 9.4. Several Russian-language forums are devoted to this simple distribution, where friendly young people will answer your most amateurish questions. Also available are lots of articles, tutorials and textbooks. We just do not forget on Google and Yandex. If your task is to learn and understand Linux, then Ubuntu will allow you to take the first step in this direction. And for those who want to have another operating system in parallel with Windows, install Ubuntu, and you just won't notice the difference.

Reasons for installing Linux:

1. Old computer, but it is a pity to throw it away and you want to work comfortably.

2. Tired of the muck from the Internet, I want a normal computer for the Internet.

3. You need to protect yourself with online commerce.

4. I am sick of spending money on computer help!

And now we will consider each item in detail:

Old computer

If your family computer is no longer young, then hung with additional protection in the face of firewall and MS Windows antivirus becomes an unbearable burden. For your protection, the firewall intercepts and processes network traffic, and the antivirus intercepts file operations for heuristic analysis and virus scan. You have to "pay" with the resources (speed) of your PC for your peace of mind.

Believe me, if you think of lightening your PC's burden and removing/disabling the firewall and antivirus, then your MS Windows will not last long.

The fact is that most Russians have pirated MS Windows and in 99% of cases cannot be updated from the microsoft.com home site and patch holes with patches that are so actively used by malware (viruses, Trojans, screwdrivers, etc.).

Experienced users know how to wriggle out of this situation when you can't easily update from the manufacturer's website but have to contrive and spin "like in a frying pan". A simple user, not having computer knowledge, remains, usually, one on one with every abomination that climbs out of the local network and the Internet, which he brings on flash drives and disks.

Installing Ubuntu Linux, you do not have to install additional protection in the face of firewall and antivirus.

Why? There are very few viruses for Linux due to the excellent system of access rights, quick fixes for vulnerabilities, proactive protection based on AppArmor security policies, centralized installation of software from trusted sources.

There is a joke that the instructions for installation and start in the system are attached to viruses in Linux.

A firewall is not required in Linux since the firewall protects open ports and doors to your computer, and in Linux, they open much less than in MS Windows. Do you not believe that? Ask an experienced friend or admin from work to show you on MS Windows in the Command Line the command: “netstat -na | findstr" LIS "| findstr / V" 127.0.0.1 "", and in Linux the command: "netstat -na | grep LIS | grep -v "127.0.0.1".

. The command will help monitor the network connections of the machine and the open ports in the state LISTEN and ESTABLISHED.

For this reason, I refused to use a firewall in Linux, when going from MS Windows, I decided to install a firewall out of habit, but then I realized that it was superfluous, and would have nothing to protect. After all, the firewall controls open ports, doors, and if there are few of them and they are controlled by programs that are controlled by proactive security policies and are updated in a timely manner, then the firewall is superfluous.

Antivirus in Linux is not needed to protect Linux, but you can install it to check for the presence of Windows viruses that are not dangerous and dangerous for Linux, and thus protect friends of MS Windows users. It is not good to spread viruses, copying folders and files with hidden viruses, and it does not matter that they are not dangerous to you. Antivirus in Linux works in “scanner” mode, not “monitor”, that is, it does not intercept file operations and does not occupy your computer's resources. Figuratively speaking, in Linux, launch the installed antivirus, check the desired file/folder/flash drive and close the antivirus program.

So! Antivirus in Linux is only needed to detect "not your own" viruses in order to stop the spread of the virus. The firewall is not required, but if you want, then "on health." It turns out in Linux at times fewer computer resources are spent on maintaining computer security. But less does not mean worse! And these are not superfluous resources you can safely use in Ubuntu Linux for safe surfing of the Internet, to watch a video.

A computer for the Internet

See what you do on your computer most of the time. If it is surfing the Internet, then Linux on your computer will fit better than MS Windows. On the Internet, computers are waiting for malicious sites, which are just waiting to get your computer and your crap out of you, exploiting various MS Windows vulnerabilities.

In the modern Internet, in order to survive, MS Windows must be additionally protected using firewalls and antiviruses. Read more about this in the “Old Computer” argument.

The fact is aggravated by the fact that the first user in MS Windows by default has unlimited administrator rights and a virus, like any other program when it arrives at the computer, it starts up with user rights. That is, in this case, with all-authoritative administrator rights. In modern versions of MS Windows such as MS Windows 7, the UAC mechanism is introduced – Control of User Accounts. It helps, but it does not solve the problem, as it is either turned off for confirming the appearance of confirmation windows. Or poking "Yes", without reading and expanding it, it is not clear to whom privileges belong.

In Ubuntu Linux, the user is not "sitting" in the system by the administrator and does not risk his security.

Many users are at great risk on the Internet in MS Windows, using Internet Explorer (this is such a blue letter E). The fact is that the majority of pirated MS Windows and many do not have the right to update from the site of the manufacturer Microsoft, but also the Internet Explorer browser is not updated either! Believe me, your old Internet Explorer browser is just happiness for virus writers and Trojans, their heart trembles with joy when such users visit sites that have exploits installed to introduce malware to you. In Germany, the authorities officially recommend not using Internet Explorer on ALL versions of MS Windows but use alternative browsers.

Installing Ubuntu Linux you will find there are such browsers as Opera, Mozilla Firefox, Google Chrome. If you used them under MS Windows, then absolutely the same versions of these remarkably secure browsers are waiting for you in Ubuntu Linux.

In MS Windows, there is a software restriction on the number of connections, so Microsoft does not allow client versions of MS Windows to “cross” the road of MS Windows Server, for example, MS Windows XP can “serve” only 10 user clients. This is necessary for Microsoft so that users do not arrange servers from home computers and do not spoil Microsoft’s business.

Read on the Internet how many people suffer with the problem, when the torrent client is started and uses many connections, it is impossible in MS Windows to comfortably surf the Internet in the browser, everything slows down. People patched the MS Windows system libraries and run the risk of the system’s performance in order to remove the software limitations on their honestly purchased computer – some horror!

There are no restrictions in Ubuntu Linux; all 65535 TCP + 65535 UDP ports are yours, there are simply no more ports! In Linux, a strong network subsystem, with settings that will be hard for you to fill up on the network, an enemy in the network under MS Windows will unload if he attacks you with some kind of network attacks.

Online Commerce

If you are using online commerce, that is, conducting financial transactions over the Internet, then Ubuntu Linux will be an excellent solution, thanks to its safety and the security of its products.

For example, the WebMoney system, in its security recommendations, writes in the first paragraphs about Linux, but regrets that you do not cope with the supposedly complicated Linux and immediately turn to MS Windows security issues.

But using Ubuntu Linux for online commerce, you can protect yourself in the same way that pirated MS Windows doesn't protect you. If you have a licensed MS Windows, then its high price will bring you closer to the security of free Ubuntu Linux. Since a huge number of viruses written under MS Windows are to steal your certificates and keys with passwords. They cannot harm your computer if you are using Ubuntu Linux.

Unfortunately, online commerce systems often release only Windows-versions of their programs for working with their system. But there is a solution! For example, for the WebMoney system, there is a mode of operation through a browser with your certificate of WebMoney Keeper Light, protected by your password and science of cryptography.

PayPal works only through the web interface. you cannot have any problems with payment systems.

Tired of spending money on computer help?!

You have to pay money for calling a computer master from your own pocket; the more you call, the more you pay. And imagine that when installing Ubuntu Linux, you get rid of this headache and do not spend money on calling specialists for many years. After all, the usual releases of Ubuntu Linux are supported for 18 months, and the long-supported release of LTS is 2 years! Put and sit quietly for two years, get updates for free. After two years, a message will appear: do you want to switch to the next LTS release? That is all!

In MS Windows, such a quiet silence is achieved by purchasing an MS Windows license and purchasing protection (firewall + antivirus) from your favorite manufacturer. In order not to pay for computer help, you must pay Microsoft and the manufacturer of protection. In general, you need to pay in MS Windows! With Ubuntu Linux you can get this for free and use on all your computers without any restrictions.

Ubuntu will always remain free, as this is one of the promises of Ubuntu.

Chapter 2 - Benefits of the Linux operating system

In this chapter, we will look at the main benefits of Linux. Here not all are collected, but the main advantages of this operating system are.

1. Linux is faster

Yes, it is. Linux kernel operating systems really benefit in terms of performance ahead of Windows. That is why the web server is most often equipped with this particular system.

Of course, not every Distributor boasts performance. For example, the world-famous Ubuntu without settings will work much worse than the same Windows 7. But there are Xubuntu and Lubuntu, which will never let you down.

2. Linux is better customizable.

Windows, as such, does not give a special leeway to take at least pre-installed tools to change the appearance. They can do little to help. But Linux!

I use the environment – am an active Linux user, programmer and founder of the ProgHacker website. Today I would like to tell you why it is worth switching to a Linux-based operating system. E of the XFCE desktop. based on this Xubutnu.

Could you do this in Windows? Maybe with the use of third-party programs, yes, but it would give significant damage to your RAM. And the above view works on a completely inconspicuous device - 1 GB OP + Pentium 4.

3. Most distributions are free.

Something I thought... But this, in fact, is a decisive factor for organizations. Almost all distributions are distributed free of charge even for commercial use. You do not need to activate, you should just download and install.

4. Linux is an open source world.

Since Linux itself is free, it has many tools built on the principle of open source software. Not only do you not have to pay for the program, but you can also make changes to them yourself. This explains the transparency of the installed programs – in the official repositories malicious software will not work.

5. Linux is safer

Linux has its roots in prehistoric UNIX systems — and since then many of the principles have remained the same. Since all the code is low-level, it does not depend on any additional libraries, it will be difficult to hack the device. And the number of Linux users is too low for hackers to pay attention as a platform for attack.

6. No need to pull hundreds of accounts

If Microsoft Windows requires the user to bind to multiple accounts, then there is no such thing in Linux. First, the account itself is optional – the number of its applications is negligible. Well, even if it is needed, almost all the services that are somehow related to Linux are tied to Ubuntu One – a single account.

7. Choose to your taste!

Are you a designer? Writer? Painter? Translator? Then, for sure, a distribution kit is ready for you, which contains all the programs ready for work!

If you had to download everything on Windows, then many Linux distributions are based on Linux that is already customized for specific needs.

For example, Ubuntu Studio is suitable for a small (or large) studio, TuxTrans for the translator, Fedora Design Suite for the artist, KXStudio for the musician.

8. Stability

If Windows requires a lot of updates, and your computer's memory is filled every six months, this will not happen in Linux. There is no registry in the usual sense of the word, and all installed packages and programs are easily controlled. So farewell, frequent reinstallation!

9. Linux weighs little

Compare Ubuntu or Xubuntu (1.8 GB and 1.3 GB respectively) with 5 GB of Windows 7. At the same time, the set of Linux programs is not only not inferior to the Microsoft product, but, on the contrary, surpasses it! The same applies to programs – they weigh significantly less.

10. Responsive community

Linux is not Windows, where you are left alone with your problem. First, there is the official English-speaking community (https://www.linux.org/forums/).

Chapter 3 - Choosing the Right Linux Distributor

There are a huge number of versions of Linux. In the history of the Linux Distributor, there were about 700 options. It is very difficult for a simple user to choose from this number. In this chapter, we will look at how to choose the right Linux Distributor for you. Let's look at what you should pay attention to when choosing a software version.

The popularity of the distribution. The more popular your distribution is, the easier it will be to find tutorials on it on the web. A large community means that you can easily get help in the forums dedicated to the distribution if you have any difficulties with its development. Finally, the more common the distribution, the more applications and packages are created for it. It is better to choose popular solutions with a ready base of packages than to suffer from the build from source in some exotic distribution.

The development command that deals with them. Naturally, it is better to pay attention to distributions supported by large companies like Canonical Ltd., Red Hat or SUSE, or to distributions with large communities.

Keep in mind that even the best Linux distributions have analogs that are not inferior to them.

Linux Mint

New users migrating from Windows definitely need to install Linux Mint. Today it is the most popular Linux distribution. This is a very stable and easy to use the system based on Ubuntu.

Linux Mint is equipped with a light and intuitive interface and a convenient application manager, so you will not have problems finding and installing programs. There are two shells: Cinnamon for modern computers and MATE for old computers. This is a very simple software that is suitable for ordinary users. You do not need any specific knowledge to install and use Mint.

There are of course disadvantages of this software. This is a large number of pre-installed programs that may never come in handy.

Manjaro

This is one of the newest Linux Distributors.

It is a popular Linux Distributor based on Arch. Arch is an incredibly powerful and functional distribution, but its KISS (Keep It Simple, Stupid) philosophy, as opposed to its name, makes it too complicated for beginners. Arch is installed only via the command line.

It, unlike Arch, has a simple graphical installer and at the same time combines the powerful features of Arch, such as AUR (Arch User Repository) and a sliding release. AUR is the richest source of Linux packages. If some application is in Linux, it probably already exists in AUR. So, in this distributor, you will always enjoy the freshest packages.

It comes with a variety of desktop shells to choose from: functional KDE, GNOME for tablet screens, Xfce, LXDE, and others. By installing this distributor, you can be sure that you get the latest updates first. This version has its own advantages of AUR, thanks to which you can install any application without unnecessary movements. Always fresh software. But, in truth, it has a peculiar design of the desktop shells. However, nothing prevents you from replacing it.

Debian

This is the distributor that is suitable for a home server. A home server can be useful for many purposes. For example, to store data and backups, upload torrents, or arrange your own dimensionless cloud storage.

This distributor will take root well on your home server. It is a stable and conservative distribution that has become the basis for Ubuntu and many other Linux systems. It uses only the most trusted packages, making it a good choice for the server. It has stability and a large set of applications. But you will have to manually configure the distribution after installation.

Kodi

This is a Linux distribution, which is suitable for a media center. If you want to build your media server, choose this distributor. Strictly speaking, it is not a distribution kit, but a full-featured media player. You can install it in any Linux, but it is best to choose a bunch of Ubuntu + Kodi.

This distributor supports all types of video and audio files. It knows how to play movies, music, organize your photos. It will turn any connected TV into a universal entertainment device.

Thanks to the extensions, it can download media files through torrents, track the appearance of new seasons of your favorite TV shows, show videos from YouTube and other streaming services. In short, Kodi can do everything.

In addition, Kodi is very beautiful and optimized for control from a remote control or device on Android. You can easily customize the Kodi interface using a variety of visual skins. It is very convenient to manage and has many functions.

But the standard interface of this may not appeal to everyone, but it is easy to replace.

There are also interesting versions: Linux distribution for desktop PC, this is Kubuntu;

A Linux distribution for an old personal computer, this is Lubuntu; The Linux version for the tablet or transformer is Ubuntu; The Linux version for the laptop is elementary OS and others.

Chapter 4 - Getting started with Linux

As for the preparation of disk space, this is the most crucial moment in the whole process of installing Linux. The fact is that if you install the system on a computer whose hard disk already has any data, then it is here that you should be careful not to accidentally lose it. If you install a Linux system on a "clean" computer or at least on a new hard disk, where there is no data, then everything is much simpler.

Why can't you install Linux in the same partition where you already have, for example, Windows, even with enough free space?

The fact is that Windows uses the FAT32 file system (in old versions – FAT16) or NTFS (in Windows NT / 2000), and in Linux, a completely different system called Extended File System 2 (ext2fs, in the newest versions – journaling extSfs). These file systems can be located only on different partitions of the hard disk.

Note that in Linux, physical hard disks are referred to as the first is hda, the second is hdb, the third is hdc, and so on (hdd, hde, hdf...).

Sometimes in the installation program of the system you can see the full names of the disks - / dev / hda instead of hda, / dev / hdb instead of hdb, and so on – this is the same thing for us now. The logical partitions of each disk are numbered. So, on a hda physical disk, there are hda1, hda2, and so on, hdb can be hdb1, hdb2, and so on. Do not be confused by the fact that these figures sometimes go in a row. It does not matter to us.

How to start installing Linux from disk

To begin installing Linux, insert the system CD into the drive and restart the computer by selecting the boot from CD. If you plan to install Linux over Windows, then the installation program can be run directly from it.

Moreover, if you are running Windows 95/98, the installation will start immediately, and if the installation program was launched from under a more powerful system, for example, Windows 2000, XP, Vista, Seven will still have to restart the computer from the CD disk.

Your computer may already be configured to boot from a CD. If the boot from the CD does not occur, when you restart your computer, enter the BIOS settings. On most systems, to do this, immediately after turning on the computer or restarting, press the Delete key or F11.

After that, find the Advanced BIOS Settings section. Sometimes the section name may be different, but in any case, it is very similar to that in this book. Enter it by first moving the pointer to it using the cursor keys and then pressing the Enter key. Now find in the parameters either the item Boot Sequence (boot order), or, if not, the item 1st boot device (first boot device). Use the cursor keys to select the desired item and, by changing its value using the Page Up and Page Down keys, make the first bootable CD-ROM device. Press the Esc key to exit the section, and then F10 to exit the BIOS with the saved settings. Most likely, the computer will ask you to confirm this intention. Usually, to confirm, you must press the Y key, which means yes.

All modern computers can boot from a CD. If for some reason your computer does not have this capability, you will have to create a boot diskette to install Linux. There are always special tools for this on the Linux distribution CD.

Usually, they are located in a folder called dos tools (or in a folder with a similar name). There are images of boot floppies and a DOS program for creating them. Read the README files on the distribution CD for more detailed instructions.

The installation of the Linux operating system can be divided into several stages:

- disk space preparation;
- selection of the programs (packages) you need;
- device configuration and graphical interface;
- install bootloader.

The installation program takes control of the entire process. You should only answer questions if the installation does not occur in fully automatic mode.

How to install Linux from a flash drive?

It often happens that if you want to install the OS, a person is faced with the fact that his drive is broken or missing. Especially often this problem happens with laptop owners. But do not be upset, because there is an alternative: installing from a Linux flash drive. To do this, you do not need a great deal of knowledge in programming, because there are special programs that "burn" the Linux image onto your USB flash drive just like on a disk. You will only need to start the installation process.

So, before you install Linux from a flash drive, you will need a flash drive with an image written onto it.

First, you should prepare the BIOS for installation.

As an example, consider installing a Linux Mint distribution. For the installation of Linux Mint from a flash drive to begin, you need to configure the startup parameters.

We insert the USB flash drive into the computer, turn it on at the very beginning, when there is a black screen on the screen and a lot of text, press the F2 button. Depending on the version of the BIOS and the computer, it may be another button – F10, Delete or Esc.

We get into the settings menu and now we need to find the "Boot" item. Again, in different versions of the BIOS it may be called differently but be guided by this word. After we have found the autorun menu, a list of priorities appears before our eyes. It contains: a hard disk, a disk drive, a removable hard disk, USB inputs, and so on. Our task is to find a flash drive in this list and put it in priority for 1 place.

It is done this way: we point the arrows at the name (for example: "USB 40GB DEVICE") and move it by pressing the F5 and F6 buttons until the USB flash drive is in 1st place.

Now the system will start the flash drive first. Press F10 and confirm the output by entering the Y (Yes) key and pressing the

Enter button.

Reboot the computer.

After that you should start the installation process.

After the computer restarts, you will see the startup menu. Often it is decorated with various images, so you will understand exactly what it is. Press Enter.

If nothing has changed or something went wrong, restart your computer and read the menu list for details. It is possible that not only the Linux installation, but also various programs are present on the recorded image.

Then you should Install it from a Linux flash drive.

All the torment behind! Already at the beginning of the installation, you will be greeted by a friendly Russian-language interface. Start by choosing a language. Select your preferred language.

Next, you need to make sure that the computer has enough free hard disk space, is connected to a power source, and is connected to the Internet. You can immediately agree that the latest updates are automatically downloaded during installation.

Click "Next." We get into the hard disk selection menu. In it, you can format and split partitions, if desired. Specify the partition (disk) in which you want to install the operating system and click the "Install Now" button.

We fall into the section change menu. Here you can increase the amount of memory, change the file system type, format the partition and specify the mount point. Use the “Ext4” file system and set the mount point “/”. If there is no valuable information on the hard disk, it is advisable to format the partition. Click "Install Now".

Now we select the country and city of residence so that the system automatically sets the time and other indicators for your personal needs. Also, specify the keyboard layout. It remains to enter the desired name for your computer, a name for the user and a password (optional). Click "Next" and start the installation process.

After the installation is complete, restart the computer, remove the USB flash drive and wait for the Linux operating system to start.

How to make a bootable USB flash drive for Linux

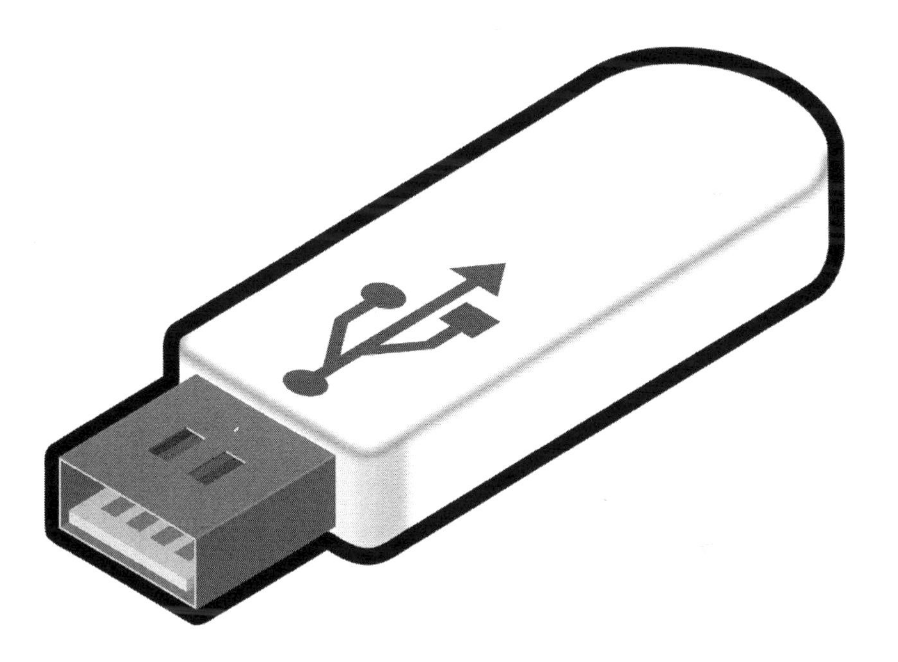

Today, the operating system is becoming increasingly popular. Surely you have already heard from your friends or acquaintances stories about how easy it is to carry out such an installation. Obviously, creating a bootable USB flash drive for Linux is a great way to reinstall the operating system on a computer with a damaged or missing drive, laptop, or netbook. Let's get acquainted with this installation method better!

First, you need to find and download a Linux operating system image.

Finding images of different versions of Linux on the Internet is very simple because it is “freeware” and is distributed absolutely free. Download the desired image on our website, official website or torrents.

A bootable Linux flash drive requires a regular flash drive. Its volume should be 1GB and higher.

Next you need to download the program Unetbootin.

This program will help us with how to make a bootable Linux flash drive. You can download it from the page unetbootin.sourceforge.net. At the top of the site there are buttons for 3 distributions – Windows, Linux and Mac OS. If you, for example, now have Windows, then press the Windows button.

After downloading, the program opens instantly, and you do not need to install it. If you have problems with the launch (Windows 7), run "on behalf of the administrator."

Initially, the program is ticked on the “Distribution”, but we need to put it on the “Disk Image”. We also indicate that this is an ISO image. Next, click on the button "..." and select the image that we previously downloaded from the Internet.

If your flash drive is capacious enough, then it is advisable to allocate space in the file storage space. 100 MB will be enough.

And at the very bottom of the program window, select which flash drive you want to burn. Example – “Type: USB drive; Media: E: \ ". If only one flash drive is inserted into the computer, the program will determine it on its own and there is no need to choose anything.

It remains only to press the "OK" button and wait until the program completes the burning of the image. It takes 5-10 minutes.

That is all you need to know about how to burn Linux to a USB flash drive. After burning, you must restart the computer or insert the USB flash drive into the computer where you want to install the Linux Operating System.

How to choose programs to install

So, the most crucial moment – the layout of the hard drive – is behind. Now the installation program proceeds to the next stage, in which it will offer to select the necessary programs (packages are traditionally called programs in Linux, which, by the way, is truer in terms of terminology).

You can simply choose one of the options for installing packages (for home computer, office, workstation with a connection to a local network, etc.). Alternatively, by turning on the Package selection switch manually, go to the software package selection window.

All programs included in the distribution of Linux are divided in this window into several sections: system, graphic, text, publishing, sound, games, documentation, and so on. In each section, you can select (or, conversely, deselect) any software package. If it is not clear from the name of the program what it is for, click on the name, and a brief description of the purpose of this program will appear in a special window. Unfortunately, in Russian-language distributions, often not all descriptions are translated into Russian, so some descriptions may be in English.

Having chosen the necessary packages for installation, be sure to locate on the screen and check the box to check dependencies. The fact is that some programs may depend on others, that is, they may use modules of other programs in their work.

Some programs may require the presence of any other software packages for normal operation. In this case, they say that one program depends on another. For example, the kreatecd CD burning program contains only a graphical user interface and calls the cdrecord console program for the actual recording, although the user doesn't see it when working.

This means that the kreatecd program depends on cdrecord. When installing Linux, all software dependencies are checked automatically; you just need to allow the installation program to do this by turning on the appropriate switch.

The checkbox for checking dependencies is needed for the installer to automatically check if some of the selected programs are using those packages that are not selected for installation. Having made such a check, the installation program will provide you with a list of these packages and will offer to install them as well. We should agree with this, otherwise, some programs will not work.

Configure devices and graphical interface

After you agree to install the necessary packages, the process of copying the necessary files to the hard disk will begin. This process is quite long, so you can go and drink coffee at this time, for at least five to ten minutes. However, if your distribution is recorded on two or more compact discs, the installer will from time to time ask you to insert the necessary compact disc into the drive.

Then the configuration of additional devices and the graphical interface will begin. There is one subtlety. The fact is that most installation programs for some reason incorrectly process information about the mouse. Therefore, the question of what kind of mouse you have at this stage is to answer a simple two-button or a simple three-button. Do not look in the list of the manufacturer, model, and so on.

After installing the system, it will be possible to separately enable additional functions of the mouse (for example, the operation of the scroll wheel) if they do not work themselves.

Install the bootloader

After all the above operations, the freshly installed system is ready for operation. However, the installer will ask you to answer one more question: should the boot loader be installed and, in most cases, if necessary, which one?

If Linux is the only operating system on your computer, then you will not need a bootloader. In this case, simply restart the computer, removing the bootable CD from it.

If you specifically changed the BIOS settings in order to allow the computer to boot from a CD or from a floppy disk, then now, after installing the system, you can reconfigure the computer to boot only from the hard disk. To do this, go back to the BIOS settings and change the boot order. However, if you specified the "universal" boot order – Floppy, CDROM, IDEO – you can no longer change it, just make sure that when you turn on and restart your computer, no boot diskettes or a CD are inserted in it, unless necessary boot from these devices.

Chapter 5 - Connecting to the Internet with Linux

Connection to the Internet is carried out using a physical channel between your computer and the provider's server.

There are three main methods for organizing a physical connection:

- wireless network;
- the local network;
- A modem through which PPP is exchanged.

In the first case, a wireless access point is required. Only if available is it possible to set up a wireless network with the

Internet.

The second method is used when your computer is connected to a local network, in which there is a server for access to the world wide web. In this case, you do not need to put your efforts into the organization of the connection – the local network administrator will do all that is necessary for you. Just launch a browser, enter the URL you are interested in, and access it.

And the third way is a dial-up modem connection. In this case, the administrator will not help you, so you have to do everything yourself. For these reasons, we decided to consider this method in more detail.

First, naturally, you should have a modem and a telephone. Next, you need to decide on the provider that provides access to the Internet and get from it the phone number by which your PC will connect to the modem pool of the provider and, of course, your username and password to access the global network.

Next, you need to configure the PPP protocol. This can be done manually, or you can use the configuration program. Manual configuration is quite complicated and requires editing files and writing scripts. Therefore, it is preferable for beginners to work with a special program that automates the entire process of setting up access to the Internet.

This program is called kppp and is originally included in the KDE graphical environment. This utility makes it much easier to set up a connection and, in most cases, requires you to only correctly specify accounting information.

Chapter 6 - Using the Shell

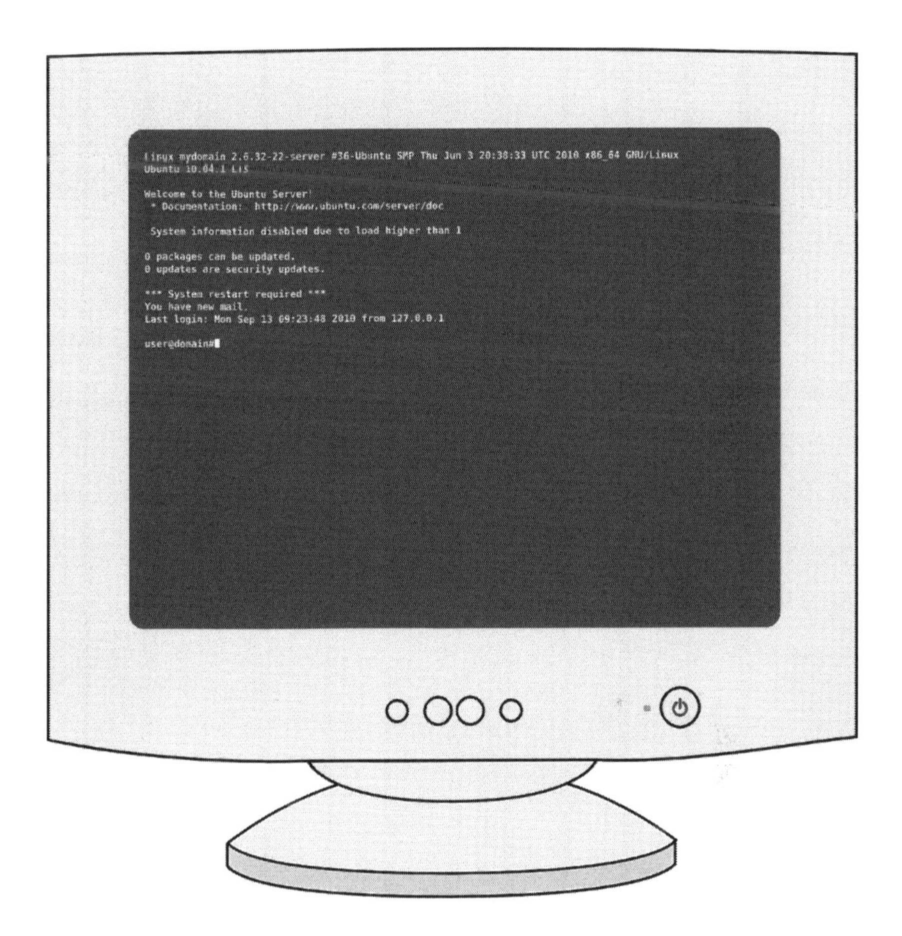

Effective Linux professional is unthinkable without using the command line.

The command line is a shell prompt that indicates the system is ready to accept a user command. This can be called a user dialogue with the system. For each command entered, the user receives a response from the system:

1. another invitation, indicating that the command is executed and you can enter the next.

2. error message, which is a statement of the system about events in it, addressed to the user.

Users who are accustomed to working in systems with a graphical interface, working with the command line may seem inconvenient. However, in Linux, this type of interface has always been basic, and therefore well developed. In the command shells used in Linux, there are plenty of ways to save effort, that is, keystrokes when performing the most common actions:

- automatic addition of long command names or file names
- searching and re-executing a command that was once performed before
- substitution of file name lists by some pattern, and much more

The advantages of the command line are especially obvious when you need to perform similar operations on a variety of objects. In a system with a graphical interface, you need as many mice dragging as there are objects, one command will be enough on the command line.

This section will describe the main tools that allow you to solve any user tasks using the command line: from trivial operations with files and directories, for example, copying, renaming, searching, to complex tasks requiring massive similar operations that occur as in the user's application work, when working with large data arrays or text, and in system administration.

Shells

A command shell or command interpreter is a program whose task is to transfer your commands to the operating system and application programs, and their answers to you. According to its tasks, it corresponds to command.com in MS-DOS or cmd.exe in Windows, but functionally the shell in Linux is incomparably richer. In the command shell language, you can write small programs to perform a series of sequential operations with files and the data they contain — scripts.

Having registered in the system by entering a username and password, you will see a command line prompt – a line ending in $. Later this symbol will be used to denote the command line. If during the installation a graphical user interface was configured to start at system boot, then you can get to the command line on any virtual text console. You need to press Ctrl-Alt-F1 - Ctrl-Alt-F6 or using any terminal emulation program, for example, xterm.

The following shells are available. They may differ depending on the distributor:

bash

The most common shell for Linux. It can complement the names of commands and files, keeps a history of commands and provides the ability to edit them.

pdkdh

The korn shell clone, well known on UNIX shell systems.

sash

The peculiarity of this shell is that it does not depend on any shared libraries and includes simplified implementations of some of the most important utilities, such as al, dd, and gzip. Therefore, the sash is especially useful when recovering from system crashes or when upgrading the version of the most important shared libraries.

tcsh

Improved version of C shell.

zsh

The newest of the shells listed here. It implements advanced features for autocompletion of command arguments and many other functions that make working with the shell even more convenient and efficient. However, note that all zsh extensions are disabled by default, so before you start using this command shell, you need to read its documentation and enable the features that you need.

The default shell is bash Bourne Again Shell. To check which shell you're using, type the command: echo $ SHELL.

Shells differ from each other, not only in capabilities but also in command syntax. If you are a novice user, we recommend that you use bash, further examples describe the work in this particular area.

Bash shell

The command line in bash is composed of the name of the command, followed by keys (options), instructions that modify the behavior of the command. Keys begin with the character – or –, and often consist of a single letter. In addition to keys, after the command, arguments (parameters) can follow – the names of the objects on which the command must be executed (often the names of files and directories).

Entering a command is completed by pressing the Enter key, after which the command is transferred to the shell for execution. As a result of the command execution on the user's terminal, there may appear messages about the command execution or errors, and the appearance of the next command line prompt (ending with the $

character) indicates that the command has completed and you can enter the next one.

There are several techniques in bash that make it easier to type and edit the command line. For example, using the keyboard, you can:

Ctrl-A

go to the beginning of the line. The same can be done by pressing the Home key;

Ctrl-u

delete current line;

Ctrl-C

Abort the execution of the current command.

You can use the symbol; in order to enter several commands in one line. bash records the history of all commands executed, so it's easy to repeat or edit one of the previous commands. To do this, simply select the desired command from the history: the up key displays the previous command, the down one and the next one. In order to find a specific command among those already executed, without flipping through the whole story, type Ctrl-R and enter some keyword used in the command you are looking for.

Commands that appear in history are numbered. To run a specific command, type:

! command number

If you enter !!, the last command typed starts.

Sometimes on Linux, the names of programs and commands are too long. Fortunately, bash itself can complete the names. By pressing the Tab key, you can complete the name of a command, program, or directory. For example, suppose you want to use the bunzip2 decompression program. To do this, type:

bu

Then press Tab. If nothing happens, then there are several possible options for completing the command. Pressing the Tab key again will give you a list of names starting with bu. For example, the system has buildhash, builtin, bunzip2 programs:

```
$ bu

buildhash builtin bunzip2

$ bu
```

Type n> (bunzip is the only name whose third letter is n), and then press Tab. The shell will complete the name and it remains only to press Enter to run the command!

Note that the program invoked from the command line is searched by bash in directories defined in the PATH system variable. By default, this directory listing does not include the current directory, indicated by ./ (dot slash). Therefore, to run the prog program from the current directory, you must issue the command ./prog.

Basic commands

The first tasks that have to be solved in any system are: working with data (usually stored in files) and managing programs (processes) running on the system. Below are the commands that allow you to perform the most important operations on working with files and processes. Only the first of these, cd, is part of the actual shell, the rest are distributed separately, but are always available on any Linux system. All the commands below can be run both in the text console and in graphical mode (xterm, KDE console). For more information on each command, use the man command, for example:

man ls

cd

Allows you to change the current directory (navigate through the file system). It works with both absolute and relative paths. Suppose you are in your home directory and want to go to its tmp / subdirectory. To do this, enter the relative path:

cd tmp /

To change to the / usr / bin directory, type (absolute path):

cd / usr / bin /

Some options for using the command are:

cd ..

Allows you to make the current parent directory (note the space between cd and ..).

cd -

Allows you to return to the previous directory. The cd command with no parameters returns the shell to the home directory.

ls

ls (list) lists the files in the current directory. Two main options: -a - view all files, including hidden, -l - display more detailed information.

rm

This command is used to delete files. Warning: deleting the file, you cannot restore it! Syntax: rm filename.

This program has several parameters. The most frequently used ones are: -i - file deletion request, -r - recursive deletion (i.e. deletion, including subdirectories and hidden files). Example:

rm -i ~ / html / *. html

Removes all .html files in your html directory.

mkdir, rmdir

The mkdir command allows you to create a directory, while rmdir deletes a directory, provided it is empty. Syntax:

mkdir dir_name

rmdir dir_name

The rmdir command is often replaced by the rm -rf command, which allows you to delete directories, even if they are not empty [26].

less

less allows you to page by page. Syntax:

less filename

It is useful to review a file before editing it; The main use of this command is the final link in a chain of programs that outputs a significant amount of text that does not fit on one screen and otherwise flashes too quickly [27]. To exit less, press q (quit).

grep

This command allows you to find a string of characters in the file. Please note that grep searches by a regular expression, that is, it provides the ability to specify a template for searching a whole class of words at once. In the language of regular expressions, it is possible to make patterns describing, for example, the following classes of strings: "four digits in a row, surrounded by spaces". Obviously, such an expression can be used to search in the text of all the years written in numbers. The search capabilities for regular expressions are very wide. For more information, you can refer to the on-screen documentation on grep (man grep). Syntax:

grep search_file

ps

Displays a list of current processes. The command column indicates the process name, the PID (process identifier) is the process number (used for operations with the process — for example, sending signals with the kill command). Syntax:

ps arguments

Argument u gives you more information, ax allows you to view those processes that do not belong to you.

kill

If the program stops responding or hangs, use this command to complete it. Syntax:

kill PID_number

The PID_number here is the process identification number, You can find out the process number for each executable program using the ps command. Normally, the kill command sends a normal completion signal to the process, but sometimes it does not work, and you will need to use kill -9 PID_number. In this case, the command will be immediately terminated by the system without the possibility of saving data (abnormal). The list of signals that the kill command can send to a process can be obtained by issuing the command kill -l.

File and Directory Operations

Here we consider utilities that work with file system objects: files, directories, devices, as well as file systems in general.

cp

Copies files and directories.

mv

Moves (renames) files.

rm

Removes files and directories.

df

Displays a report on the use of disk space (free space on all disks).

du

Calculates disk space occupied by files or directories.

ln

Creates links to files.

ls

Lists files in a directory, supports several different output formats.

mkdir

Creates directories.

touch

Changes file timestamps (last modified, last accessed), can be used to create empty files.

realpath

Calculates absolute file name by relative.

basename

Removes the path from the full file name (i.e., shortens the absolute file name to relative).

dirname

Removes the file name from the full file name (that is, it displays the full name of the directory where the file is located).

pwd

Displays the name of the current directory.

Filters

Filters are programs that read data from standard input, convert it and output it to standard output. Using filtering software allows you to organize a pipeline: to perform several sequential operations on data in a single command. More information about standard I / O redirection and the pipeline can be found in the documentation for bash or another command shell. Many of the commands listed in this section can work with files.

cat

combines files and displays them to standard output;

tac

combines files and displays them on standard output, starting from the end;

sort

sorts rows;

uniq

removes duplicate lines from sorted files;

tr

performs the replacement of certain characters in the standard input for other specific characters in the standard output, can be used for transliteration, deletion of extra characters and for more complex substitutions;

cut

systematized data in text format can be processed using the cut utility, which displays the specified part of each line of the file; cut allows you to display only the specified fields (data from some columns of the table in which the contents of the cells are separated by a standard character — a tabulation character or any other), as well as characters standing in a certain place in a line;

paste

combines data from several files into one table, in which the data from each source file make up a separate column;

csplit

divides the file into parts according to the template;

expand

converts tabs to spaces;

unexpand

converts spaces to tabs;

fmt

formats the text in width;

fold

transfers too long text lines to the next line;

nl

numbers file lines;

od

displays the file in octal, hexadecimal and other similar forms;

tee

duplicates the standard output of the program in a file on disk;

Other commands

head

displays the initial part of the file of the specified size;

tail

outputs the final part of a file of a given size, since it can output data as it is added to the end of the file, used to track log files, etc.;

echo

displays the text of the argument on the standard output;

false

does nothing, comes out with a return code of 1 (error), can be used in shell scripts if an unsuccessful command is being attempted;

true

does nothing, comes out with a return code of 0 (successful completion), can be used in scripts if a successful command is required;

yes

infinitely prints the same line (by default, yes) until it is interrupted.

seq

displays a series of numbers in a given range of successively increasing or decreasing by a specified amount;

sleep

suspends execution for a specified number of seconds;

usleep

suspends execution for a specified number of milliseconds;

comm

compares 2 pre-sorted (by the sort command) files line by line, displays a table of three columns, where in the first are lines unique to the first file, in the second are unique to the second, in the third they are common to both files;

join

combines lines of two files on a common field;

paste

For each pair of input lines with the same common fields, print the line to standard output. By default, the general field is considered first, the fields are separated by whitespace.

split

splits the file into pieces of a given size.

Calculations

In addition to simple operations with strings (input/output and merging), it is often necessary to perform some calculations on the available data. Listed below are utilities that perform calculations on numbers, dates, strings.

test

returns true or false depending on the value of the arguments; The test command is useful in scripts to check conditions;

date

displays and sets the system date, in addition, it can be used for calculations over dates;

expr

evaluates expressions;

md5sum

calculates checksum using MD5 algorithm;

sha1sum

calculates checksum using SHA1 algorithm;

wc

counts the number of lines, words, and characters in the file;

factor

decomposes numbers into prime factors;

Search

The search for information in the file system can be divided into a search by file attributes (understanding them extensively, that is, including the name, path, etc.) and content search. For these types of search, the programs find and grep are usually used, respectively. Thanks to convenient interprocess communication tools, these two types of search are easy to combine, that is, to search for the necessary information only in files with the necessary attributes.

Attribute search

The main search tool for file attributes is the find program. A generalized call to find looks like this: find path expression, where path is a list of directories in which to search, and expression is a set of expressions that describe the criteria for selecting files and the actions to be performed on the files found. By default, the names of found files are simply output to standard output, but this can be overridden and the list of names of found files can be transferred to any command for processing. By default, find searches in all subdirectories of directories specified in the path list.

Expressions

Expressions that define file search criteria consist of key-value pairs. Some of the possible search options are listed below:

-amin, -anewer, -atime

The time of the last access to the file. Allows you to search for files that were opened for a certain period of time, or vice versa, for files that nobody has accessed for a certain period.

-cmin, -cnewer, -ctime

The time the file was last changed.

-fstype

The type of file system on which the file is located.

-gid, -group

User and group that owns the file.

-name, -iname

Match the file name to the specified pattern.

-regex, -iregex

Match the file name to a regular expression.

-path, -ipath

Match the full file name (with the path) to the specified pattern.

-perm

Access rights.

-size

File size.

-type

File type.

Actions

The find program can perform various actions on the found files. The most important of them are:

-print

Output the file name to the standard output (the default action);

-delete

delete a file;

-exec

execute the command by passing the file name as a parameter.

You can read about the rest in the on-screen documentation for the find command, by issuing the man find command.

Options

Parameters affect the overall behavior of find. The most important of them are:

-maxdepth

maximum search depth in subdirectories;

-mindepth

minimum search depth in subdirectories;

-xdef

Search only within the same file system.

You can read about the rest in the on-screen documentation for the find command.

Terminals

The terminal in Linux is a program that provides the user with the ability to communicate with the system using the command line interface. Terminals allow you to transfer to the system and receive only text data from it. The standard terminal for the Linux system can be obtained on any textual virtual console, and in order to access the command line from the graphical shell, special programs are needed: terminal emulators. Listed below are some of the terminal emulators and similar programs included in the ALT Linux 2.4 Master distribution.

xterm

Programs: resize, uxterm, xterm.

Standard terminal emulator for the X Window System. This emulator is compatible with DEC VT102 / VT220 and Tektronix 4014 terminals and is designed for programs that do not use the graphical environment directly. If the operating system supports changing the terminal window (for example, a SIGWINCH signal on systems that have gone from 4.3bsd), xterm can be used to inform programs running on it that the window size has changed.

aterm

Aterm is a color emulator of the terminal rxvt version 2.4.8, supplemented with NeXT-style scroll bars by Alfredo Kojima. It is intended to replace the xterm if you do not need a Tektronix 4014 terminal emulation.

console-tools

Programs: charset, chvt, codepage, consolechars, convkeys, deallocvt, dumpkeys, fgconsole, "" setkeycodes, setleds, setmetamode, setvesablank, showcfont, showkey, splitfont, unicode_stop, vcstime, vt-is-UTF8, writevt.

This package contains tools for loading console fonts and keyboard layouts. It also includes a variety of fonts and layouts.

In case it is installed, its tools are used during boot / login to establish the system / personal configuration of the console.

screen

The screen utility allows you to execute console programs when you cannot control their execution all the time (for example, if you are limited to session access to a remote machine).

For example, you can perform multiple interactive tasks on a single physical terminal (remote access session) by switching between virtual terminals using a screen installed on a remote machine. Or this program can be used to run programs that do not require direct connection to the physical terminal.

Install the screen package if you may need virtual terminals.

vlock

The vlock program allows you to block input when working in the console. Vlock can block the current terminal (local or remote) or the entire system of virtual consoles, which allows you to completely block access to all consoles. Unlocking occurs only after successful authorization of the user who initiated the console lock.

Chapter 7 - Moving around the File system

Work with file systems. Let us take a closer look at what can be done with file systems.

Mounting File Systems

Before the file system becomes available to the operating system, it must be mounted (mounted) in a directory. For example, if there is a file system on a diskette, then in order to provide access to its files, it must be mounted, for example, in the / mnt / floppy directory — this directory is called the mount point. After mounting this file system, all its files are in the appropriate directory. After unmounting the file system, this directory will be empty.

The same applies to file systems on the hard disk. The so-called root file system (root file system) is mounted in the / directory. If there is a separate / home file system, it is mounted in the / home directory. If there is only a root file system, then all files (including those that are in the / home directory) are only in it. The operating system automatically mounts file systems located on hard disks during boot. File systems on removable media (such as floppy disks, CD-ROMs, etc.) are also mounted in most cases automatically using the automount program.

Mount and umount programs (not unmount) are used to mount and unmount file systems. The mount -av command runs automatically during system boot. Information about file systems and mount points can be located in the / etc / fstab file. An example of the / etc / fstab file is shown below.

device directory type options

(device) (directory) (type) (options)

#

/ dev / hda1 / ext3 defaults

/ dev / hda2 / home ext3 defaults

/ dev / cdrom / mnt / cdrom auto user, noauto, ro

/ dev / hda4 none swap swap

/ proc / proc proc none

The first field (device) contains the name of the partition to be mounted. The second field is the mount point. The third field is the file system type, auto here means that the file system type should be determined automatically. The last field contains mount options. Often, they are installed by default (defaults). In the above example, the user option indicates that the file system can be mounted by a regular user (usually this is a superuser privilege), noauto means that the file system will not be mounted automatically when it is loaded. Learn more about mount options in the mount screen documentation. The following file system types are supported in ALT Linux 2.4 Master.

Ext2

It is the most traditional for Linux and the most stable of all available file systems; however, it is not journaling, i.e., in the event of a power outage, etc., all information that has not been written to disk will be lost and errors may occur in the file system. Therefore, after a failure, it is necessary to check the file system with fsck.

Ext3

Ext2 development with journaling support; well compatible with Ext2. Ext2 can be easily converted to Ext3 using the tune2fs -j / dev / hdXN command. For the inverse transformation, it is enough to mount this section as Ext2.

Reiserfs

A journaling system optimized for directories containing many files, as well as for small files. Version 3.6 for 2.4.x kernels is recommended for use at this time.

ISOFS

Used on CD-ROM media.

UDF

Used on DVD-ROM media.

VFAT

Used in Microsoft Windows 9x, Microsoft Windows 2000 operating systems.

NTFS

Used in Microsoft Windows NT, Microsoft Windows XP operating systems. Currently, only readable file systems of this type are supported.

The ISOFS and UDF file systems are used in CD / DVD-ROM media; VFAT and NTFS are used by the Microsoft operating system family.

The file / etc / fstab also includes information on swap sections. They have a mount point of none (i.e., not mounted) and the type swap.

The / etc / fstab file contains one special entry for the / proc file system. This file system contains information about the processes running in the system, available memory, etc. If the / proc partition is not mounted, then commands like ps will not work.

File system check

In the Master, the check of file systems for the presence of damaged files is performed automatically at boot time if necessary, and also regularly for preventive purposes. However, sometimes you need to manually start the check: for this it is enough to issue the fsck / dev / hdXN command, and it will automatically detect the type of file system being scanned and run the necessary command.

Before checking the file system, it is useful to unmount it, and if the fsck program will make any repairs to the file system, then it must be done.

Chapter 8 - Working with the Text Files

Text filtering is the process of obtaining an input text stream, performing some transformations on it, and transferring the changed data to the output stream. Although input or output data may come from files, in UNIX® and Linux, filtering is usually done by composing pipelines from commands in which the output of one command is transmitted through a programming channel (or redirected) to the input of the next command. Program channels and redirections are discussed in more detail in the article “Flows, program channels and redirections” (see the list of materials for preparing for examinations for LPIC-1), and now let’s look at program channels and simple output redirections using operators | and>.

Streams

A stream is just a sequence of bytes that can be read or written using library functions that hide implementation and operation details of devices from applications. The same program can read or send data to a terminal, file, or network location using streams, regardless of the device used. In modern programming environments and command interpreters, three standard streams are used:

• stdin - standard input stream (input stream), which provides input for commands.

• stdout — standard output stream, which displays the results of command execution.

• stderr - standard error stream (standard error stream), which provides the display of errors that occur when executing commands.

Pipelined using operator |

The parameters passed to the commands can serve as input to these commands, and the output can be output to your terminal. Many text processing commands (filters) can receive input from either standard input or a file. To pass the output of command 1 to input command 2 (acting as a filter), you need to connect these two commands with an input/output pipeline (|) operator. Example 1 shows how to redirect the output of the echo command to the input of the sort command, which sorts the resulting list of words.

Example 1. Transfer echo command output to sort command input

```
1 [ian@echidna ~]$ echo -e "apple\npear\nbanana"|sort
2 apple
3 banana
4 pear
```

Any of these commands may have options or arguments. With the help of the operator | you can also redirect the output of the second command to the input of the third team, and so on. Building long pipelines from teams, each of which has its own limited functionality, is a technique common in Linux and UNIX that is used to solve the set tasks. Sometimes the command argument may not be a file name, but a hyphen (-) character; This means that the input data should be taken from a standard input device, and not from a file.

Redirecting output using the> operator

Of course, it is good to be able to create pipelines from several commands and display the results on the terminal screen, but sometimes it becomes necessary to save the output to a file. To do this, use the output redirection operator (>).

In the remaining examples of this article, we will use small files, so let's create a directory named lpi103-2 and go into it. After that, let's redirect with the help of the> operator the output of the echo command to a file named text1. These actions are shown in Example 2. Note that since all the output is redirected to a file, it is not displayed on the screen.

Example 2. Redirecting command output to a file

```
1 [ian@echidna ~]$ mkdir lpi103-2
2 [ian@echidna ~]$ cd lpi103-2
3 [ian@echidna lpi103-2]$ echo -e "1 apple\n2 pear\n3 banana" > text1
```

Now that we have several tools for pipelining and redirection, let's look at a few text processing commands and filters common to Linux and UNIX. In this section, you will be introduced to some of the main teams. For more information about them, refer to the corresponding man pages.

Cat, od and split commands

Once you have created the test1 file, you can view its contents. To output the contents of a file to a standard output device, use the cat command (short for concatenate - combine). Example 3 displays the contents of the file we just created.

Example 3. Displaying the contents of a file using the cat command

```
1 [ian@echidna lpi103-2]$ cat text1
2 1 apple
3 2 pear
4 3 banana
```

If you do not specify a file name (or put a hyphen instead of a file name), then the cat command accepts input from a standard input device. Let's use this feature (as well as output redirection) to create another text file, as shown in example 4.

Example 4. Creating a text file with the cat command

```
1 [ian@echidna lpi103-2]$ cat >text2
2 9     plum
3 3     banana
4 10    apple
```

Other simple filters

Another example of a simple filter is the tac command (the inverted name of the cat command). This command performs the action of the cat commands the other way around. The lines of the file are displayed in reverse order. Try running the following command yourself:

tac text2 text1

In Example 4, the cat command continues to read data from the stdin device until the end of the file is reached. To mark the end of the file, press Ctrl-d (hold Ctrl and press d). The same key combination is used to exit the bash command interpreter. Use the tab key to line up the names of the fruits in the column.

Have you forgotten that cat is short for concatenating? With cat, you can combine several files and display their contents on the screen. Example 5 shows the contents of the two files that we created.

Example 5. Combining two files with the cat command

```
1 [ian@echidna lpi103-2]$ cat text*
2 1 apple
3 2 pear
```

```
4 3 banana
5 9     plum
6 3     banana
7 10    apple
```

Notice the different alignment of the contents of the two text files when they are displayed on the screen with cat. To understand why this happens, you need to look at the control characters that are present in the files. These characters affect the text output, but do not have a visual display, so you need to create a dump file in a format that allows you to see and identify these special characters. GNU-utility od (Octal Dump) is intended for this purpose.

The od command has several options; for example, the -A option controls the basis of the file offset, and the -t option controls the form of the output. The base can be specified as o (octal, used by default), d (decimal), x (hexadecimal) or n (no offsets are displayed). You can output the contents as octal, hexadecimal, decimal, floating-point values, ASCII characters with escape sequences, or named characters (nl for a newline, ht for horizontal tabs, etc.). Example 6 shows several available dump2 formats for the text2 file from our example.

Example 6. File dumps created using the od command

```
   [ian@echidna lpi103-2]$ od text2
1  0000000 004471 066160 066565 031412 061011 067141
2  067141 005141
3  0000020 030061 060411 070160 062554 000012
4  0000031
5  [ian@echidna lpi103-2]$ od -A d -t c text2
6  0000000  9 \t  p  l  u  m \n  3 \t  b  a  n  a  n  a \n
7  0000016  1  0 \t  a  p  p  l  e \n
8  0000025
9  [ian@echidna lpi103-2]$ od -A n -t a text2
10  9 ht  p  l  u  m nl  3 ht  b  a  n  a  n  a nl
11  1  0 ht  a  p  p  l  e nl
```

The files used in our examples are very small, but sometimes you may encounter large files that need to be divided into several smaller ones. For example, you may need to split one large file into several pieces so large that they can be burned onto CDs. To do this, you can use the split command, which splits files in such a way that they can later be easily assembled back into a single file using the cat command. By default, the names of files created by the split command consist of the prefix 'x', followed by the suffix 'aa', 'ab', 'ac', ..., 'ba', 'bb', and so on. These defaults can be changed using various options. You can also set the size of the output files and determine whether they will contain a certain number of lines or just have a certain size in bytes.

Example 7 shows the separation of our two text files using different prefixes for the output files. We divided the text1 file into files with a maximum of two lines, and the text2 file into files with a maximum size of 18 bytes. Then, using the cat command, we displayed some separate parts, as well as the entire file, using the universalization of file names.

Example 7. Sharing and restoring files using the split and cat commands

```
1  [ian@echidna lpi103-2]$ split -l 2 text1
2  [ian@echidna lpi103-2]$ split -b 17 text2 y
3  [ian@echidna lpi103-2]$ cat yaa
4  9     plum
5  3     banana
6  1[ian@echidna lpi103-2]$ cat yab
7  0     apple
8  [ian@echidna lpi103-2]$ cat y* x*
9  9     plum
10 3     banana
11 10    apple
12 1 apple
13 2 pear
14 3 banana
```

Notice that the file named yaa does not end with a new line, so when we displayed its contents on the screen with the cat command, our invitation moved to the right.

Wc, head, and tail commands

The cat command displays the full contents of the file. This works well for small files (for our examples), but what if the file size is very large? So, for starters, you can estimate the file size using the wc command (Word Count). The wc command displays the number of lines and words in the file, as well as the file size in bytes, which can also be determined using the ls -l command. Example 8 shows a detailed display of information about our two text files, as well as the output of the wc command.

Example 8. Using the wc command to work with text files

```
1 [ian@echidna lpi103-2]$ ls -l text*
2 -rw-rw-r--. 1 ian ian 24 2009-08-11 14:02 text1
3 -rw-rw-r--. 1 ian ian 25 2009-08-11 14:27 text2
4 [ian@echidna lpi103-2]$ wc text*
5  3  6 24 text1
6  3  6 25 text2
7  6 12 49 total
```

Various options allow you to control the output of the wc command or display other information, such as the maximum string length. See the man page for more information.

The other two commands allow you to display either the first part of the file (header) or the last (tail). These commands are called head and tail, respectively. You can use them as filters or pass them the name of a file as an argument. By default, these commands display the first 10 (or last) lines of a file or stream. In Example 9, the dmesg (display of system boot information), wc, tail, and head commands are shared; as a result, we see that the file contains 791 messages, displays the last 10 of them, and then displays six messages, starting from 15 from the end.

Example 9. Using the wc, head, and tail commands to display boot messages

```
   [ian@echidna lpi103-2]$ dmesg|wc
     791   5554  40186
   [ian@echidna lpi103-2]$ dmesg | tail
   input:            HID            04b3:310b           as
   /devices/pci0000:00/0000:00:1a.0/usb3/3-2/3-2.4/3-
   2.4:1.0/input/i
   nput12
   generic-usb 0003:04B3:310B.0009: input,hidraw1: USB HID
 1 v1.00 Mouse [HID 04b3:310b] on us
 2 b-0000:00:1a.0-2.4/input0
 3 usb 3-2.4: USB disconnect, address 11
 4 usb 3-2.4: new low speed USB device using uhci_hcd and
 5 address 12
 6 usb 3-2.4: New USB device found, idVendor=04b3,
 7 idProduct=310b
 8 usb 3-2.4: New USB device strings: Mfr=0, Product=0,
 9 SerialNumber=0
10 usb 3-2.4: configuration #1 chosen from 1 choice
11 input:            HID            04b3:310b           as
12 /devices/pci0000:00/0000:00:1a.0/usb3/3-2/3-2.4/3-
13 2.4:1.0/input/i
14 nput13
15 generic-usb 0003:04B3:310B.000A: input,hidraw1: USB HID
16 v1.00 Mouse [HID 04b3:310b] on us
17 b-0000:00:1a.0-2.4/input0
18 usb 3-2.4: USB disconnect, address 12
19 [ian@echidna lpi103-2]$ dmesg | tail -n15 | head -n 6
20 usb 3-2.4: USB disconnect, address 10
21 usb 3-2.4: new low speed USB device using uhci_hcd and
22 address 11
23 usb 3-2.4: New USB device found, idVendor=04b3,
24 idProduct=310b
25 usb 3-2.4: New USB device strings: Mfr=0, Product=0,
```

```
SerialNumber=0
usb 3-2.4: configuration #1 chosen from 1 choice
input:              HID             04b3:310b             as
/devices/pci0000:00/0000:00:1a.0/usb3/3-2/3-2.4/3-
2.4:1.0/input/i
nput12
```

Another common use of the tail command is file tracking. To do this, use the -f option and step, usually equal to one line. This can be useful if you have a background process that generates output to a file, and you want to monitor its progress. In this mode, the tail command will work and output lines as they are added to the file until you finish it by pressing Ctrl-c.

Expand, unexpand, and tr commands

When we created our text1 and text2 files, the last one used tabs. Sometimes you may need to replace tabs with spaces and vice versa. For this purpose, the commands expand and unexpand. In both commands, the -t option allows you to set tab stops. If only one value is specified after this option, then tab stops will be placed periodically at this specified interval. Example 10 shows how to reduce the tabs in the text2 file to single spaces, and also shows a bizarre sequence from the expand and unexpand commands and violates the alignment of text in the text2 file.

Example 10. Using the expand and unexpand commands

```
1 [ian@echidna lpi103-2]$ expand -t 1 text2
2 9 plum
3 3 banana
4 10 apple
5 [ian@echidna lpi103-2]$ expand -t8 text2|unexpand -a -
6 t2|expand -t3
7 9     plum
```

```
8|3       banana
 |10      apple
```

Unfortunately, you cannot use the unexpand command to replace spaces in the text1 file with tabs, since the unexpand command requires at least two consecutive spaces to convert to a tabulation character. However, you can use the tr command, which converts characters from one set (set1) into corresponding characters from another set (set2). Example 11 shows an example of using the tr command to convert spaces to tabs. Since the tr command is a pure filter, the input to it is generated using the cat command. This example also shows an example of using a hyphen (-) to indicate that input will be from a standard device; thus, we can combine the output of the tr command with the contents of the text2 file.

Example 11. Using the tr command

```
1|[ian@echidna lpi103-2]$ cat text1 |tr ' ' '\t'|cat - text2
2|1     apple
3|2     pear
4|3     banana
5|9     plum
6|3     banana
7|10    apple
```

If you do not really understand what is happening in the last two examples, then try using the od command to execute each command of the pipeline sequentially, for example:

```
cat text1 | tr '' '\ t' | od -tc
```

Pr, nl, and fmt commands

The pr command is used to format files before printing. By default, the header includes the file name, the date and time the file was created, the page number, and two empty footer lines. When data comes from multiple files or from a standard input device, the current date and time is used instead of the date and time the file was created. You can print files side by side, each in its own column, as well as manage many of the formatting options using various options. As usual, additional information can be found on the man page.

The nl command numbers lines, which can be useful when printing files. You can also use the cat command with the -n option to number lines. Example 12 shows how to print our text file, number the lines in the text2 file, and print it with the text1 file.

Example 12. Numbering lines and formatting before printing

```
1  [ian@echidna lpi103-2]$ pr text1 | head
2
3
4  2009-08-11 14:02                    text1                    Page 1
5
6
7  1 apple
8  2 pear
9  3 banana
10
11
12 [ian@echidna lpi103-2]$ nl text2 | pr -m - text1 | head
13
14
15 2009-08-11 15:36                                             Page 1
16
17
18      1 9     plum                   1 apple
19      2 3     banana                 2 pear
20      3 10    apple                  3 banana
```

Another useful command for formatting text is the fmt command, which formats the text so that it does not go beyond the boundaries of the fields. You can combine several short lines into one long line and vice versa. In Example 13, we created a text3 file using a single long construct of combinations of characters! #: * (Designed to control the history of commands), so that the printed sentence was saved in the file four times. We also created a text4 file containing one word per line. Then, using the cat command, we displayed the contents of these files in an unformatted format, including the end of the line '$'. Finally, we used the fmt command to format these files, limiting the maximum string length to 60 characters. As usual, additional information can be found on the man page.

Example 13. Formatting with maximum line length

```
   [ian@echidna lpi103-2]$ echo "This is a sentence. " !#:* !#:1-
   >text3
   echo "This is a sentence. " "This is a sentence. " "This is a
1  sentence. ">text3
2  [ian@echidna lpi103-2]$ echo -e
3  "This\nis\nanother\nsentence.">text4
4  [ian@echidna lpi103-2]$ cat -et text3 text4
5  This is a sentence.  This is a sentence.  This is a sentence. $
6  This$
7  is$
8  another$
9  sentence.$
10 [ian@echidna lpi103-2]$ fmt -w 60 text3 text4
11 This is a sentence.  This is a sentence.  This is a
12 sentence.
13 This is another sentence.
```

Sort and uniq commands

The sort command sorts the input data using the locale ordering scheme (LC_COLLATE) of the system. The sort command can also merge already sorted files and determine whether the file is sorted or not.

Example 14 shows examples of using the sort command to sort two text files after replacing spaces with tabs in the text1 file. Since the sorting is based on character values, you might be surprised to see the results. Fortunately, the sort command can sort not only based on character values but also based on numeric values. You can specify the required sorting method for the entire record or for each field. If you do not specify a field delimiter, spaces or tabs are used. In the second example of example 14, the first field is sorted by numeric values, and the second field is sorted using an ordering scheme (in alphabetical order). An example of using the -u option to remove duplicate lines is also shown.

Example 14. Sorting by character and numeric values

```
   [ian@echidna lpi103-2]$ cat text1 | tr ' ' '\t' | sort - text2
1  10    apple
2  1     apple
3  2     pear
4  3     banana
5  3     banana
6  9     plum
7  [ian@echidna lpi103-2]$ cat text1|tr ' ' '\t'|sort -u -k1n -k2 -
8  text2
9  1     apple
10 2     pear
11 3     banana
12 9     plum
13 10    apple
```

Note that the list still contains two lines with the word "apple", since the uniqueness check was performed on all the sort keys (in our case, it is k1n and k2). Think about what commands you need to change or add to the pipeline in the last example to eliminate duplication of the word 'apple'.

You can control the removal of duplicate lines with another command, uniq. In normal mode, the uniq command works with sorted files and removes consecutive duplicate lines from any file, regardless of whether it is sorted or not. Also, this command can ignore the specified fields. In Example 15, our two text files are sorted by the second field (fruit name), after which the lines in which the second field values are repeated (that is, we do not pay attention to the first field during the check).

Example 15. Using the uniq command

```
[ian@echidna lpi103-2]$ cat text1|tr ' ' '\t'|sort -k2 - text2|uniq -
1 f1
2 10    apple
3 3     banana
4 2     pear
5 9     plum
```

In this example, the sorting was performed using the ordering scheme, so the uniq command left the entry "10 apple" rather than "1 apple". You can add the sorting of the first field by numeric values and see what changes in this case.

Chapter 9 - Sed Editor

Sed (stream editor) is a stream editor. Sed is an extremely powerful tool, and the range of tasks it solves is limited only by your imagination. This short review should pique your interest in sed, although it is not complete and comprehensive.

Like many text commands we've reviewed here, sed can act as a filter or accept input from a file. The output is carried out on a standard output device. Sed loads the lines from the input data into the template area, applies editing commands to its contents, and sends it to the standard output device. Sed can merge several lines in the template area; the result can be written to a file, it can be written partially, or it can be not recorded at all.

For search and selective replacement of text in the template area, as well as to determine the lines on which you need to perform certain editing commands, sed uses regular expression syntax. A temporary storage of text is a retention buffer. The hold buffer can replace the template area with itself, can be added to the template area, and can exchange data with it. Although sed has a limited number of commands, using them together with regular expressions and the hold buffer opens unlimited possibilities. A set of sed commands is usually called a sed script.

Example 16 shows three simple sed scripts. In the first scenario, the s (substitute - replace) command is used to replace the lower-case character 'a' in each line with the same upper-case character. In the first example, only the first character 'a' is replaced, so in the second example we added the flag 'g' (global - global), thanks to which, all found occurrences of this character will be replaced. In the third scenario, we use the d (delete) command to delete a line. In our example, we used address 2 to show that you only need to delete the line with this number. We separate the commands with a semicolon (;) and use the global substitution of the characters 'a' for 'A', as was done in the second example.

Example 16. First steps in working with sed scripts

```
1  [ian@echidna lpi103-2]$ sed 's/a/A/' text1
2  1 Apple
3  2 peAr
4  3 bAnana
5  [ian@echidna lpi103-2]$ sed 's/a/A/g' text1
6  1 Apple
7  2 peAr
8  3 bAnAnA
9  [ian@echidna lpi103-2]$ sed '2d;$s/a/A/g' text1
10 1 apple
11 3 bAnAnA
```

In addition to working with individual lines, sed can work with a range of lines. The beginning and end of the range are separated by a comma (,) and can be defined as a line number, a regular expression, or a dollar sign ($) meaning the end of the file. Knowing the address or range of addresses, you can group several commands by enclosing them in curly braces {and}; thus, these commands will work only with those lines that are specified in the range. Example 17 shows two examples of global replacements that apply only to the last two lines of our file. An example of using the -e option to add several commands to a script is also given.

Example 17. Addresses in sed

```
1  [ian@echidna lpi103-2]$ sed -e '2,${' -e 's/a/A/g' -e '}' text1
2  1 apple
3  2 peAr
4  3 bAnAnA
5  [ian@echidna lpi103-2]$ sed -e '/pear/,/bana/{' -e 's/a/A/g' -e '}' text1
6  1 apple
7  2 peAr
8  3 bAnAnA
```

Sed scripts can be saved as files. Most likely, you will want to use this feature for the most frequently used scenarios. Recall the tr command that we used to change the spaces in the text1 file to tab characters. Let's now do the same with the sed script stored in the file. To create the file, we use the echo command. The results are presented in example 18.

Example 18. Short sed program

```
1 [ian@echidna lpi103-2]$ echo -e "s/ /\t/g">sedtab
2 [ian@echidna lpi103-2]$ cat sedtab
3 s/ /	/g
4 [ian@echidna lpi103-2]$ sed -f sedtab text1
5 1	apple
6 2	pear
7 3	banana
```

There are many similar short scenarios.

In our last example, we first use the = command to print the line numbers, and then we filter the output by using sed (as a result we get the same effect as using the nl command to number the lines). In Example 19, the line number is displayed using the = command, then the second input line is read into the template area using the N command, and finally, the new line character (/ n) is deleted between the two lines in the template area.

Example 19. Numbering strings with sed

```
1  [ian@echidna lpi103-2]$ sed '=' text2
2  1
3  9      plum
4  2
5  3      banana
6  3
7  10     apple
8  [ian@echidna lpi103-2]$ sed '=' text2|sed 'N;s/\n//'
9  19     plum
10 23     banana
11 310    apple
```

Not exactly what we wanted to get! In fact, we expected to get an aligned column with line numbers, followed by the file lines themselves, separated by several spaces. In Example 20, we enter several lines with commands (note the additional> prompt). Study this example and read its explanation below.

Example 20. Numbering strings with sed, another option

```
1  [ian@echidna lpi103-2]$ cat text1 text2 text1 text2>text6
2  [ian@echidna lpi103-2]$ ht=$(echo -en "\t")
3  [ian@echidna lpi103-2]$ sed '=' text6|sed "N
4  > s/^/     /
5  > s/^.*\(......\)\n/\1$ht/"
6       1 1 apple
7       2 2 pear
8       3 3 banana
9       4 9      plum
10      5 3      banana
```

```
11     6 10     apple
12     7 1 apple
13     8 2 pear
14     9 3 banana
15    10 9      plum
16    11 3     banana
17    12 10     apple
```

Here is what was done in this example:

1. First, using the cat command, we created a file containing 12 lines of two copies of the text1 and text2 files (if the number of lines was less than 10, i.e. all the numbers were of the same order, then there would be no point in formatting them).
2. In the bash command interpreter, the tab key is used to complete a command, so it is convenient to have a predefined tab character for use when you need it. To do this, using the echo command, we saved the tab character in the 'ht' environment variable.
3. We created a stream containing the line numbers and the next data lines as we did before, and filtered it with the second copy of sed.
4. We read the second line in the template area.
5. At the beginning of the template area (denoted by the ^ symbol) we added a prefix consisting of six spaces to the line number.
6. Finally, we applied alignment using a separator containing the last six characters and a tab, and now the line numbers in the output will be aligned to the first six characters. Note that on the left side of the 's' command, the '\ (' and '\)' constructs are used to mark the characters that we

want to use on the right side. In the right part, we refer to the first (and only in our example) such set of characters using / 1. Note that our command is enclosed in double quotes ("), so this substitution will be done for the $ ht variable.

The latest (fourth) version of the sed editor contains documentation in the info format and includes many excellent examples. In the older version, 3.02, these features are missing. You can find out the version of the GNU sed editor using the sed --version command.

Chapter 10 - Managing Running Processes

Processes. The system calls fork () and exec (). Thread.

A process in Linux (as in UNIX) is a program that runs in a separate virtual address space. When a user logs into the system, a process is automatically created in which the shell is executed, for example, / bin / bash.

Linux supports the classic multiprogramming scheme. Linux supports parallel (or quasi-parallel if there is only one processor) user processes. Each process runs in its own virtual address space, i.e. processes are protected from each other and the collapse of one process will not affect the other running processes and the system as a whole. One process cannot read anything from the memory (or write to it) of another process without the "permission" of another process. Authorized interactions between processes are allowed by the system.

The kernel provides system calls for creating new processes and for managing generated processes. Any program can start executing only if another process starts it or some interruption occurs (for example, an external device interrupt).

In connection with the development of SMP (Symmetric Multiprocessor Architectures), a mechanism of threads or control threads was introduced into the Linux kernel. A thread is a process that runs in virtual memory, used together with other threads of a process that has separate virtual memory.

If the shell encounters a command corresponding to the executable file, the interpreter executes it, starting from the entry point. For C programs, the entry point is a function of main. A running program can also create a process, i.e. run some program and its execution will also begin with the function main.

Two system calls are used to create processes: fork () and exec. fork () creates a new address space that is completely identical to the address space of the main process. After executing this system call, we get two identical processes: the main and the generated ones. The fork () function returns 0 in the spawned process, and the PID (Process ID is the spawn of the spawned process) basically. PID is an integer.

Now that we have already created the process, we can start the program by calling exec. The exec function parameters are the name of the executable file and, if necessary, the parameters that will be passed to this program. A new program will be loaded into the address space of the fork () process and will start from the entry point (the address of the main function).

As an example, consider this fragment of the program.

if (fork () == 0) wait (0);

else execl ("ls", "ls", 0); / * spawned process * /

Now let's take a closer look at what happens when you execute a fork () call:

1. Memory is allocated for the new process handle in the process table.

2. Assign process ID PID.

3. A logical copy of the process is created that performs fork () – full copying of the virtual memory contents of the parent process, copying the components of the nuclear static and dynamic contexts of the ancestor process.

4. Increase the file opening counters (the child process inherits all open files of the parent process).

5. Returns the PID to the return point from the system call in the parent process and 0 in the descendant process.

General process control scheme.

Each process can spawn a completely identical process using fork (). The parent process can wait until all its descendant processes have completed executing using the wait system call.

At any time, a process can change the contents of its memory image using one of the exec call types. Each process responds to signals and, of course, can set its own response to signals produced by the operating system. The priority of the process can be changed using the nice system call.

A signal is a way of informing the core process of the occurrence of an event. If several events of the same type occur, only one signal will be sent to the process. A signal means that an event has occurred, but the kernel does not report how many such events have occurred.

Examples of signals:

1. termination of the child process (for example, due to the exit system call (see below))

2. the occurrence of an exceptional situation

3. signals from the user when you press certain keys

You can set the response to a signal by using the signal system call.

func = signal (snum, function);

snum is the signal number, and function is the address of the function to be executed when the specified signal arrives. The return value is the address of the function that will respond to a signal. Instead of function, you can specify zero or one. If a zero was specified, then when the snum signal arrives, the process will be interrupted similarly to the exit call. If you specify a unit, this signal will be ignored, but it is possible

For normal completion of the process call is used.

exit (status);

where status is an integer returned by the ancestor process to inform it about the reasons for the termination of the descendant process.

The exit call can be set at any point in the program, but it can also be implicit, for example, when exiting the main function (when programming in C), the operator return 0 will be interpreted as the system call exit (0);

input / output Redirection

Virtually all operating systems have an input/output redirection mechanism. Linux is no exception to this rule. Usually, programs enter text data from the console (terminal) and output data to the console. When you enter the console means the keyboard, and then output, the terminal display. The keyboard and display are standard input and output (stdin and stdout), respectively. Any input/output can be interpreted as input from a file and output to a file. Work with files is done through their descriptors. UNIX uses three files for input/output: stdin (handle 1), stdout (2), and stderr (3).

The> symbol is used to redirect standard output to a file.

Example:

$ cat> newfile.txt The standard input of the cat command will be redirected to the file newfile.txt, which will be created after the execution of this command. If a file with this name already exists, it will be overwritten. Pressing Ctrl + D will stop the redirect and abort the execution of the cat command.

The <symbol is used to reassign standard command input. For example, if you run the cat <file.txt command, the file.txt file will be used as standard input, not the keyboard.

The >> symbol is used to append data to the end of the file (append) of the standard command output. For example, unlike the case with the symbol>, the execution of the command cat >> newfile.txt will not overwrite the file if it exists but will add data to its end.

Symbol | is used to redirect the standard output of one program to the standard input of another. For example, ps -ax | grep httpd.

Process Management Commands

Ps command

Designed to display information about running processes. This command has many parameters that you can read about in the manual (man ps). Here I will describe only the most frequently used commands:

- ✓ "a" display all processes associated with the terminal (all user processes are displayed)
- ✓ "e" show all processes
- ✓ "t" terminal list, display terminal-related processes
- ✓ "u" user identifiers, display the processes associated with these identifiers
- ✓ "g" group IDs, display the processes associated with these group IDs.
- ✓ "x" display all non-terminal processes

Program "top"

Designed to display information about processes in real time. Processes are sorted by maximum CPU time, but you can change the sort order (see man top). The program also reports free system resources.

top

7:49 pm up 5 min, 2 users, load average: 0.03, 0.20, 0.11

56 processes: 55 sleeping, 1 running, 0 zombie, 0 stopped

CPU states: 7.6% user, 9.8% system, 0.0% nice, 82.5% idle

Mem: 130660K av, 94652K used, 36008K free, 0K shrd, 5220K buff

Swap: 72256K av, 0K used, 72256K free 60704K cached

PID USER PRI NI SIZE RSS SHARE STAT% CPU% MEM TIME COMMAND

1067 root 14 0 892 892 680 R 2.8 0.6 0:00 top

1 root 0 0 468 468 404 S 0.0 0.3 0:06 init

2 root 0 0 0 0 0 SW 0.0 0.0 0:00 kflushd

3 root 0 0 0 0 0 SW 0.0 0.0 0:00 kupdate

4 root 0 0 0 0 0 SW 0.0 0.0 0:00 kswapd

5 root -20 -20 0 0 0 SW <0.0 0.0 0:00 mdrecoveryd

You can view information about RAM with the help of the free command, and about the disk memory - df. Information about users registered in the system is available using the w command.

Changing process priority useful command

nice [-reduction factor] command [argument]

The nice command executes the specified command with a lower priority, the reduction factor is specified in the range 1..19 (by default it is equal to 10). The superuser can increase the priority of the command. For this you need to specify a negative factor, for example - --10. If you specify a coefficient greater than 19, then it will be considered as 19.

nohup - ignore interrupt signals

nohup command [argument]

nohup runs a command in the ignore mode. Only the SIGHUP and SIGQUIT signals are not ignored.

kill - forced completion of the process

kill [signal number] PID

where PID is the process identifier that can be found using the ps command.

Commands for running processes in the background - jobs, fg, bg

The jobs command lists the processes that run in the background, fg - puts the process in normal mode ("to the foreground" - foreground), and bg - in the background. You can run the program in the background using the <command> &

Conclusion

Currently, the user of a personal computer has a wide range of operating systems.

Leading software manufacturers have made sure that the end user gets the most loyal and convenient way to work with a personal computer.

Until recently, it was believed that Linux-based operating systems were quite difficult to manage and are suitable only for "confident" users. Is it so?

We should start with the fact that now on the market there are three of the largest companies developing software. This is

1. Microsoft, and its Windows

2. Apple and its Mac OS

3. Linux and Linux distributions (the most popular is Ubuntu).

Note that the first two systems are paid software and their price starts from a few hundred dollars. Unlike Windows and Mac OS, Linux distributions are completely free.

It is also worth noting that Mac OS is distributed exclusively with Apple products. In other words, personal computer users cannot install this operating system. Only Mac computer and laptop owners can install this.

In addition to pricing, Linux also benefits from system security and stability. All of us have heard stories that a dangerous virus has appeared on the network, which can delete all the data of Windows users. For UNIX systems, viruses are practically non-existent.

Downloading from the Internet or ordering a free disk with the Ubuntu distribution, you will receive a fully-fledged operating system.

You will not need to download additional software: all the basic applications required for the average user are already included in the Ubuntu package.

I hope, that you really enjoyed reading my book.

Thanks for buying the book anyway!

Printed in Great Britain
by Amazon